The
Flowering
Southwest

The

Flowering
Southwest

WILDFLOWERS, CACTI and SUCCULENTS
in Arizona, California, Colorado,
Nevada, New Mexico, Texas and Utah

Paintings by Erni Cabat
Text by Rodney G. Engard

TUCSON, ARIZONA

Published by:
GREAT IMPRESSIONS
an imprint of Great Arts Press, Inc.
55 West Adams, Suite 210
P.O. Box 65270
Tucson, Arizona 85740-2270
(602) 882-5100

ISBN 0-925263-00-1   Printed in U.S.A.
Library of Congress Catalog Number: 89-80187   10 9 8 7 6 5 4 3 2 1

Designed by Burton Design.
Edited by Michael Rule.
Lithography on acid-free 80-lb. Warren's Lustro Dull by Fabe Litho, Ltd.
Binding by Roswell Bookbinding.

Contents

Contents

Preface

All life is shaped by environment. The plants presented here face severe challenges from climate and terrain, and their adaptations have produced forms and behaviors that stretch the limits of believing.

Some grow without blooming for forty years and then, in the course of a few weeks or months, raise a twenty-foot stalk of flowers. Some bloom only at night; by dawn, the flowers close, never to reopen. A huge subterranean tuber puts a handful of sticks above the surface while a nearby cactus squats on the ground like a barrel, making do with only a thin webbing of roots. Some species form sweet fruits to attract the creatures that will broadcast their seeds; others lace their tissues and fluids with deadly toxins.

Many are armed. Their hooks, barbs, thorns, spikes and needles make them seem invulnerable, but the plants in fact represent a delicate balance between supply and demand in a land where there is never quite enough.

The greatest threat, though, is from human activity. As this book went to press, the bats largely responsible for pollinating Saguaros, agaves and Organ Pipes appeared for the first time on the U.S. Fish and Wildlife Endangered Species List. According to the Federal Register, the future of the bats is in question because people are killing them and eliminating their roosting sites and food sources.

And without the bats, the plants are in peril. The lesson is clear: the arid Southwest is a place of magic, but, like all magic, it is fragile, something to be respected and treated with care.

Michael J. Rule
Editor

to
kepi lonis

———

Flower Face

Cacti and Succulents

Succulents, including the cacti, make up an estimated 3 or 4 percent of the flowering plants of the world. While aboriginal peoples often use them for food, materials and medicine, they do not contribute greatly to the economic well-being of mankind. A horticultural industry has developed around the plants but, though locally important, the world economy does not rise or fall on "succulents futures."

Why then do they attract such an inordinate amount of attention wherever they are displayed? Simply put, the plants are among the most bizarre on the planet. Their colors, forms and adaptations to harsh environments have fired the imagination of mankind since Rome was in the ascendancy. The Age of Discovery brought new and strange botanical wonders from India, Africa and the New World to the attention of scholars, and fascination with the plants flourished among the wealthy of Europe. There are Cactus and Succulent societies all over the world, crossing political and ideological barriers bridged by few other interests.

Many different families of flowering plants have evolved succulent members. The plants cover a wide range of climate, habit and habitat. They are trees, shrubs, herbs and annuals. They are at home in steamy jungles, high pine forests, cool alpine meadows and torrid deserts.

What is a succulent?

Succulence is an adaptation to the vagaries of a variable environment. The simplest and broadest definition of a succulent is that it is a plant which stores water in its tissue for later use, against the chance that the environment will be dry for some portion of the year or, in extreme cases, longer. This is a rather loose notion of succulence, though, and an impressively diverse list results when it is applied to the plant kingdom as a whole. So the bulbs, tubers and those plants with thickened roots have been excluded; these are seen as food-storage organs rather than moisture-saving adaptations. The exclusion is somewhat arbitrary and not universally accepted.

What to include or exclude among peripheral groups of plants is something of a personal judgment; presented here are representatives of all of the traditional major groups which have known succulent members in the flora of the Sonoran Desert.

By far the most widely known of these plant groups is the cactus family, the Cactaceae.

What is a cactus?

Often, casual observers do not distingush between the botanical "cactus" and the other spiny desert-adapted plants. There are some 2,000 cacti, or cactuses; with the possible exception of one species, all are native to the Western Hemisphere. But members of this family are very adaptable; having escaped cultivation they have become naturalized in many warmer regions of the world. Many times, indigenous peoples in these areas have grown up with the plants and believe them to be native because of the local lore and uses that have evolved since their introduction.

So what makes a plant a cactus? Very simply, it is the presence of a structure called an areole, no matter how minute or disguised. Cacti are characterized by having stems of wildly differing shapes, from elongate to flat to spherical or cylindrical. The stems may or may not have ribs or the protruberances called tubercles. The surfaces of all, however, are dotted at regular intervals with a peculiar tuft of hair, or spines, or both. Known as areoles, these structures are entire branch systems; the leaves are reduced to spines of various sizes and configurations or to mere hairs, and the whole branch is telescoped into a pad or tuft. All flowering, fruiting and branching takes place from these structures or, in one case, from the vessels that supply nutrition to the area of the areole. Sometimes the areole is divided into two portions some distance from one another.

The spines on cacti serve several functions. The most obvious is that they protect the plants from animals which might otherwise find them palatable or a source of moisture in an arid environment. Spineless or minimally spined cacti have highly refined and effective chemical systems for the same purpose. Spines also shade the plant to a great degree from the high radiation allowed by nearly cloudless skies.

On some cacti, ribs also provide shade. Ribs additionally allow the plants to expand and contract like accordions without doing physical damage as water is gained or lost during the course of the seasons.

Ground temperatures in some habitats may reach 170 degrees F on summer days, while the air temperature is only 110 or so. During these periods the plants may simply shut down their gas exchange with the environment, an option which would be lethal to many non-adapted plants.

To reduce evaporation, stems have thick waxy coatings called cuticle.

Most of our native cacti have shallow spreading roots which enable them to absorb even slight amounts of moisture. Larger species also have deep tap roots for support.

Although mature cacti often grow in open spaces and in garden-like settings, they start as seedlings hidden beneath the canopy of desert trees, shrubs or other cacti. The seedlings are ill-adapted to withstand the full blast of the environment. The plants under which they find succor are known as nurse plants.

Cactus and Succulent Growth Regions

	Arizona	California	Colorado	Nevada	New Mexico	Texas	Utah
Saguaro or Giant Cactus	■						
Soaptree Yucca	■				■	■	
Arizona Queen-of-the-Night	■				■	■	
Ocotillo	■	■			■	■	
Engelmann's Hedgehog	■						
Jumping or Chainfruit Cholla	■						
Purple Prickly Pear	■						
Wislizen's Barrel Cactus	■	■				■	
Cork or Sponge-seed Pincushion	■						
Organ Pipe Cactus	■						
Diamond Cholla	■	■		■			
Buckhorn Cholla	■	■		■			■
Beavertail Cactus	■	■		■			■
Golden-flowered Century Plant	■						
Sotol or Desert Spoon	■			■			
Arizona Rainbow Cactus	■				■		
Pencil Cholla	■						
Flame Flower	■				■	■	
Sea Purslane	■	■		■	■	■	
Desert Hen-and-Chicks	■	■					
Rusby's Hen-and-Chicks	■						

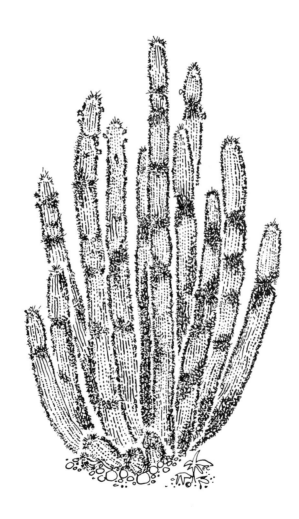

Saguaro or Giant Cactus

The Saguaro or Giant cactus is more than the bearer of the Arizona state flower. To people around the world, it is the living symbol of the North American deserts. In fact, though, it is limited to the Sonoran Desert of southern Arizona and the adjoining Mexican state of Sonora.

The plants are massive; they can grow to fifty feet, and may weigh several tons. Flowering occurs at the tips of the main stem and arms of mature plants. While most flowers appear in May, a few develop as late as August, after the summer rains. The flowers are white with thick, shining petals. Three inches across and four inches long, the flowers open at night but often remain open the next day.

Pollination occurs as at least two species of migratory bats from Mexico forage in the blossoms for food. The nectar and pollen provide the bats with a proper diet of sugars, proteins, vitamins and minerals. During the day, many insects and birds, particularly the White-winged Dove, also visit the flowers to gather pollen and nectar.

Developing in June and July, the fruit is scaly and shaped like elongated eggs, two to three inches long. A few short wiry spines project from under the scales. As the fruit ripens its color changes from green to green suffused with red or pink. When fully mature the fruit splits open irregularly along two or three longitudinal fissures, revealing the scarlet-red interior. Embedded in the pulp is a mass of shiny blackish seeds, each a sixteenth of an inch long. The fruit is extremely sweet and nutritious; the pulp is high in sugars and very tasty, and the seeds are stuffed with protein and oil.

The Pima, Tohono O'odham and other desert-dwelling tribes use the Saguaro extensively for food and other purposes. The Tohono O'odham and Pima calendar years begin with the sagauro harvest. In the cool hours of early morning women and children gather the ripe fruit, dislodging it from the tall plants with a rod made of saguaro ribs. The afternoon is spent boiling the fruit; the end products are dried pulp, seeds, syrup and jam.

At the end of the collecting season, a communal Saguaro Wine Festival is held in some villages even today. Rising from a rich tradition of ritual songs and oratory, the ceremony calls down the summer rains which are essential to the unirrigated crops maintained by these peoples.

Even in death the Saguaro provides material useful to desert dwellers. Woody, strong and light, their ribs are used for roofing ramadas, and the walls of homes were often made of mud, plastered onto wattles made of saguaro ribs.

Many birds, from Cactus Wrens to owls and hawks, nest in the crooks formed by the upthrust branches of mature plants. Many also fatten on the seeds and pulp or on the insects attracted to the ripening fruit, and small mammals eat the fruit which falls to the ground.

Saguaro or Giant Cactus   Cactaceae   *Cereus giganteus*

The Gila Woodpecker is an exceptional resident because it actually excavates nesting holes in the trunks and branches. The holes rarely do permanent damage; Saguaros normally produce a corky scar tissue to line the round-bottomed cavity. The scar tissue is more resistant to decay than the surrounding tissue; once the plant has died and toppled, the nests remain lying on the desert, often encased in a temporary prison of saguaro ribs. Because of their characteristic shape, the nests are known locally as "saguaro boots" and are prized by flower arrangers and others.

Even after the woodpeckers have abandoned their nests in the living plant, other birds use them to hide from predators and the desert heat. Among these are dwarf owls and the ubiquitous Starling.

Many beliefs surround the Saguaro. The Tohono O'odham have several concerning the plant's origin, centering on the belief that the cacti were all people at one time and thus deserve respect, if not reverence. Another legend is the purported great age of the plants. Some may live for 300 years, but, since growth rings are not formed as in most trees, accurate ages cannot be determined. The number of branches is of no help; some Saguaros never branch, while others may start five or more branches in a single year.

As with all cacti, Saguaros are protected by law.

Fruiting Saguaro

Soaptree Yucca

Soaptree Yucca is one of the commonest of Southwestern plants. It is also among the most visible; the sight of its flowering stalks standing against the clear blue sky is strikingly dramatic. It is the state flower of New Mexico.

The plant is most abundant on sandy-gravel plains and wide-bottomed valleys throughout central and southeastern Arizona and southern New Mexico. The stems grow in dense or sparse clumps. Most are less than twelve feet high; rarely, specimens grow to twenty feet. Topping each stem is a dense rosette of several hundred thin leaves, eighteen inches to three feet long. The leaves are flexible and have threads, sharp tips and white margins. Orioles use the threads to build nests among the dried leaves. The leaves turn tan as they dry but cling to the stems for many years.

In April, flower stalks emerge from the axils of leaves near the actively growing apex of the stem. The stalks grow to two inches in diameter and twelve feet long, with lateral branches along the upper half to two-thirds of their lengths. The flowers are three inches long, creamy white and shaped like bells. Each flower has six petal-like parts. The plants were formerly placed among the lilies, but the flowers betray them as members of the Century Plant family.

The first flowers are fully formed by June; flowering continues through July. The plants are pollinated by female moths of the genus *Tegeticula* (formerly *Pronuba*). For more on this fascinating relationship, see the Appendix.

Yuccas rank high among the useful plants of the Southwest. For at least 2,000 years the leaves of many species have produced fiber for ropes, twine, sandals, nets, coarse cloth and baskets. Brooms and brushes have been made from the leaves and fiber. Detergent for washing hair and clothing has been derived from the powdered roots and rhizomes.

Modern uses include shampoos, cleansing powders, toothpastes and powders, medicines, nutritional supplements and fertilizer. During extreme droughts the stems have been used for livestock feed. The Pueblo Indians of New Mexico even fashion birdcages from the leafy heads. Before the introduction of flint and steel, the stalks were used to make the fireboards and drills necessary to make fire. All of the species are ornamental and many are common in cultivation.

Soaptree Yucca   Agavaceae   *Yucca elata*

Arizona Queen-of-the-Night

La Reina de la Noche is also known as the Night-Blooming-Cereus, but that name describes many species of cactus and is therefore of little use. The fabled fragrance and beauty of the Queen-of-the-Night is not betrayed by the vegetative portions of these plants, offering as they do one of the most inconspicuous and least attractive aspects of any of our native cacti.

The above-ground portion of the plant consists of one or more slender, fluted gray stems. These are covered with very fine dense hairs and have four to eight more-or-less prominent ribs. The ribs bear rows of areoles with short spines that lay close to the surface. Stems may reach eleven feet if supported on other vegetation, but three-foot stems or less are average.

The weak, poorly developed spines offer little protection from the browsing of thirsty desert herbivores, and the plant normally grows with its cluster of dry dead-looking stems thrust up among the branches of shrubs or trees. The camouflage is almost perfect; this is one of its secrets of survival. Another major survival adaptation is the large quantities of food and moisture stored in the fleshy tuber-like root. Shaped like rutabagas, these roots may weigh up to a hundred pounds and yet have only one or a few spindly stems marking their presence. The roots are edible raw or cooked but are not particularly tasty.

The real surprise comes on evenings in June or July. At about ten o'clock, the fully developed buds, six to eight inches long, begin to open with a series of spasmodic jerks. By two o'clock, the white (or, rarely, pink) flower is fully open. The flowers close early the following morning and never reopen.

Flowers may be five inches across when fully open. The narrow tube flares as it ascends and the pointed strap-shaped petals cascade and recurve like spider mums, but much more densely. The fragrance is a musky perfume which scents the air for a quarter of a mile downwind, though some people are unable to detect any scent at all.

The fruit is two to four inches long, scarlet-red and elliptical. It is edible, but birds usually find it first and devour the dull black seeds through a hole pecked in the side of the fruit. They distribute the seeds widely, usually at the base of a nurse plant upon which they have perched.

The plants are much more common than is supposed. Typical habitats are sand and gravel flats among creosote bushes and in the brush growing along the margins of dry washes. The plants are found in the southern half of Arizona and in the desert regions of New Mexico, Texas, California and Mexico.

Arizona Queen-of-the-Night   Cactaceae   *Peniocereus greggii*

Ocotillo

The Ocotillo is a member of the Candlewood family, which has only fourteen species and varieties, all native to Mexico or the southwestern United States. Among these, only one species has a range which extends into the United States; it occurs in southwest Texas, New Mexico, California, Nevada and Arizona. Habitat varies greatly; Ocotillos grow naturally at elevations from near sea level to 5,000 feet, in low deserts and on gentle mountain slopes and ridges.

Ocotillos are classified as drought-deciduous stem-succulents. This means that water is stored in the stems during moist periods; during drought, the leaves become a liability because they lose water to the atmosphere. The plants simply drop the leaves, quickly revegetating when conditions of abundant moisture return.

The relatively shallow, spreading roots support a short trunk which in turn branches into many long, slender, wand-like stems. The overall outline is that of a funnel standing on its spout. The plants may be up to thirty feet high with trunk diameters of over eighteen inches; the individual stems are slender, usually less than an inch and a half thick at the middle. Each stem is protected by a close-set spiral of grayish spines half an inch to an inch long. The spines are derived from the hardened lower portion of the leaf stalks, called petioles, of the initial leaves. Later leaves are without petioles and form dense clusters at the bases of the spines.

Ocotillos are most handsome in the spring and summer, when bright green leaves obscure the spines and when showy pennants, six to twelve inches long, wave from the tips of mature branches. The pennants are clusters of orange-red tubular flowers that produce abundant sweet nectar, attracting hummingbirds and bees. Unable to descend the narrow tube of some varieties, the bees obtain nectar by making a vertical slit in the flower tube above the sepals to insert their mouth parts. With their long bills, hummingbirds can feed directly. The fruit is a three-part brown capsule which splits open to reveal five to eighteen seeds, each covered by a mass of white hairs. The seeds are edible, but not very palatable.

In the early days, the long straight stems were used as roofing materials for houses and ramadas; traditionalists among several Arizona and Mexican Indian peoples continue the practice. Even today impenetrable fences are made by planting the cut stems in rows, so close together that they touch. The cuttings take root and become a living green fence which may even flower in good seasons. At the turn of the century a superb boot dressing was manufactured from the waxy cuticle of the stems. The plants are now protected by law and are a popular accent plant in arid-land landscapes.

Ocotillo   Fouquieriaceae   *Fouquieria splendens*

Engelmann's Hedgehog

There are a number of species and varieties of hedgehog cacti in the Southwest. They vary from small single-stemmed plants to plants forming dense, many-stemmed mounds a foot or more high and four feet wide.

Hedgehogs are unusual among cacti because flowers occur above a mature areole rather than from within it. Flowering occurs in the area of past growth, down the stem from the apex. The buds form beneath the surface of the stem rib and burst through the skin as they swell and grow. Each flower leaves behind a telltale scar on the stem after it fades or develops into a fruit.

Engelmann's Hedgehog is very common throughout the western and southern half of Arizona, in one or more of its five recognized varieties, at elevations up to 5,000 feet. The areoles are round and bear four to six central spines, flattened at the base. Other hedgehogs have fewer central spines or none at all.

Between three and sixty erect stems form clusters up to two feet high and a yard wide. Each stem is from an inch and a half to three inches in diameter and bears ten to thirteen ribs. Flowers are purplish-magenta to lavendar, two to two and a half inches in diameter. The shimmering intensity of the colors makes this one of our most dramatic March and April wildflowers.

The fruits are edible when ripe, and are claimed by some to taste like strawberries, though the comparison seems to deprecate the flavor of strawberries. The areoles on these scarlet to orange-red fruits bear clusters of spines which fall off as the fruit ripens, allowing animal disseminators ready access to the seed. The plant was named after Dr. George Engelmann, who was the director of Henry Shaw's famed Missouri Botanical Garden.

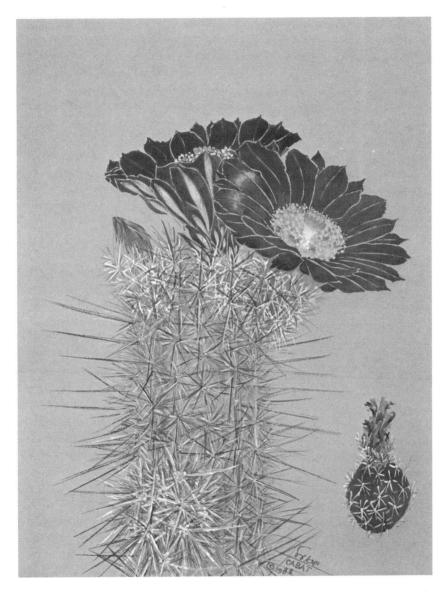

Engelmann's Hedgehog   Cactaceae   *Echinocereus engelmannii*

Jumping or Chainfruit Cholla

Jumping Cholla is among the most annoying and painful desert plants. The stems are covered with barbed spines which in turn are covered with a barbed papery sheath. At the slightest touch, the stem detaches and lodges painfully into flesh or clothing. The plants are a particular bane to pet owners.

The plants form dense forests of single-trunked shrubs or small trees up to fifteen feet high. Stems are cylindrical, an inch and a half to two inches in diameter, attached in clusters at the tips of two to five blackened main branches. The best way to remove offending stems is to lift them off two-handedly with a pair of ordinary hair combs, but the papery spine sheath is brittle, and even when the spine is removed, the sheath may remain behind to itch, pain and fester.

There are two varieties: the common one, silvery and with many spines, and Boxing Glove Cholla, *Opuntia fulgida* var. *mammillata*, which is greenish and has fewer spines.

The flowers are pink with five to eight petals and white-lobed stigmata. As is usual with cacti, there are many stamens. Each successive flowering occurs from areoles at the free edge of the previous year's fruit; remaining green and attached for many years, the fruit forms long chains, hanging in bunches like clusters of grapes. The fruits separate if the cluster itself is detached.

The tan seeds in each fruit are hard and bony and are difficult to germinate. If not eaten by rodents, the fruits become partially buried; roots grow from the buried areoles and shoots form a new plant, genetically identical to the parent.

The limbs are a haven for many species of desert birds. Most notable are the Cactus Wren and several species of thrasher. The birds hop about the plants busily building nests or caring for their young, oblivious to the needle-like spines. Few predators will brave these fortresses to attack the nestlings. Two that do are the Red Racer and the Whipsnake, which are protected by their own scaly armor.

Little horticultural use of these plants is made because of the danger the spines present to small children.

Jumping or Chainfruit Cholla   Cactaceae   *Opuntia fulgida*

Purple Prickly Pear

The Purple Prickly Pear gets its name not from the color of its flowers, which are yellow, but from the color of the stem joints. Often called pads, stem joints are round, flattened stems. The purple color is derived from chemicals, called betalains, that are dissolved in the cell sap. The same type of pigments are found in beets, and result here in a similar though less intense color. The color intensifies during periods of cold or drought and is most pronounced in young, growing joints.

The plant is a medium to large shrub with a short trunk and oval pancake-shaped joints four to seven inches in diameter. These pads may or may not bear robust spines from the uppermost areoles on the edge of the plant.

Four varieties are recognized, all from southern Arizona and adjacent areas in and near desert grassland at elevations of 3,000 to 5,000 feet. It is sometimes known as Santa Rita Prickly Pear after the Santa Rita Mountains, just south of Tucson.

Since it is dry when ripe, the fruit is useless for eating or jelly-making, both traditional uses of prickly pear fruit. Nor are the stems edible as *nopalitos,* the diced cactus stems served as a Southwestern vegetable.

Purple Prickly Pear   Cactaceae   *Opuntia violacea*

As the name implies, the barrel cactus is usually shaped like a barrel: columnar and flat-bottomed when mature. The tops are rounded. Branching is not rare, but, unless they have been injured, Wislizen's Barrels are normally unbranched. The roots grow only from the central core of the plants and fan out just beneath the surface of the soil.

The Wislizen's Barrel is very common throughout the southern half of Arizona. Sometimes mixed with other barrels, they occur on the gravelly slopes, mesas and plains surrounding Tucson and Phoenix at elevations up to 5,000 feet. They are also found in California and Texas.

The cacti are distinguished by a combination of bright orange-yellow or orange-red flowers, ribs which spiral up the stem and central spines that are usually flattened, hooked or curved with ridges running across them. Flowering occurs from areoles some distance out from the growing apex of the stem, forming a ring of blossoms like a crown. Each flower consists of many narrow, pointed petals nestled in a protective sanctuary of spines.

The flowers are pollinated by insects; the fruit is bright yellow, spineless and with fleshy scales. The seed escapes from a pore at the base of the fruit. Birds eat the seeds and desert deer and other mammals eat the fruit, which is generally considered too mucilaginous and astringent for human consumption.

In the lore of the arid Southwest, no plants figure more prominently than do the barrel cacti. All plants contain very high percentages of water in their tissues; barrel cacti are no exception. Old stories tell of lives saved by the water and, while some of the stories are true, a fuller recounting is due.

Some Indian groups lived in parts of the Sonoran Desert where the springs and seeps were unreliable and the watercourses were usually rivers of dry sand. Flood water would sometimes be trapped in depressions eroded into the bedrock, but that was not dependable either. When all else failed, moisture could be obtained from some barrel cacti for short periods.

To get to the rubbery core, the spines were burned away and the top was cut off, or the plant was removed bodily from the ground and split open lengthwise. Pounding and crushing the core released the mucilaginous liquid. But the juice contains toxic alkaloids which, depending on the concentration, cause severe nausea and other side effects. Drinking the fluid was an act of desperation.

Another tale of the desert is that the plants always lean to the south or southwest, toward the stronger and longer exposure to light from these directions. Hence, the name Compass Barrel is applied to some species. On open plains this is often the case, but soil texture, slope exposure and shading by nearby plants and rocks intervene and make the plants unreliable as direction indicators.

Wislizen's Barrel Cactus   Cactaceae   *Ferocactus wislizenii*

Cork or Sponge-seed Pincushion

This little plant has a single stem three to six inches long and up to two and a half inches across. The stems are fleshy or flaccid rather than firm. Like all pincushion cacti, the areole is divided into two parts: a spineless portion at the base of a conical projection of the stem called a tubercle, and a spine-bearing portion at the tip of the tubercle. It is found at elevations below 2,500 feet in Mexico, western Arizona and adjoining states.

The white radial spines are so numerous and dense that they nearly obscure the body of the plant. There are from one to four robust central spines, blackish and hooked. A few straight, slender central spines may also be present.

The rosy pink flowers are about an inch across. Flowering occurs only on the older portions of the stem some distance from the apex and only from the spineless basal portion of the areole.

Known locally as *chilitos* or "little chilis," the bright red fruits are about an inch long and up to a half-inch wide. Found within are the seeds that give the plant its common names. Each spherical black seed is about a twelfth of an inch in diameter; attached to the base of each seed is a swollen corky or spongy three-lobed mass of white or brown tissue called an aril. It is supposed that the aril holds scarce moisture near the emerging root, thus aiding the seedling's slender chance of survival. The fruits are edible, but little worth the effort as they are never abundant.

Cork or Sponge-seed Pincushion   Cactaceae   *Mammillaria tetrancistra*

Organ Pipe Cactus

Organ Pipe cacti are very common in western Mexico. In the United States they are restricted to the Organ Pipe Cactus National Monument and its environs south of Ajo, Arizona, and to a few other isolated locations in south-central Arizona.

The plants may be up to twenty feet high and nearly as wide. As the common name suggests, the stems curve upward from ground level or from a short trunk until they are all erect and parallel, like the pipes of an organ.

The dark green stems are four to eight inches in diameter and pleated with twelve to twenty ribs. Running along the crests of the ribs are close-set areoles with brittle gray, black or brown needle-like spines. The bases of growing spines are bright pink and soft.

Flowers are pale pink, two to three inches in diameter. The flowers are nocturnal but often remain open the following day. As with Saguaros, the most reliable pollination is by nectar-feeding bats. The fruit is a very shiny red sphere, three inches in diameter when ripe; as the fruit ripens, the spines become deciduous and fall off.

The Spanish name, *pitahaya dulce,* is a corruption of an Indian name and refers to a sweet edible cactus fruit. The Tohono O'odham regarded organ pipe fruit as even more palatable than saguaro fruit, although the question is open. In coastal Sonora, Mexico, the Seri Indians used the stem wood for torches and the mucilaginous pulp to make pitch to caulk their boats.

The plants are quite striking but are rarely cultivated because of their low availability and inability to withstand periodic prolonged frost.

Organ Pipe Cactus   Cactaceae   *Stenocactus (Cereus* or *Lemaireocereus) thurberi*

Diamond Cholla

It is little wonder that Diamond Cholla has taken on an armed and armor-plated appearance; it grows in the most inhospitable of climates. The plant is native to the low desert on both sides of the Colorado River from southern Utah to Mexico, at elevations between 100 and 3,000 feet. In this harsh environment, the clumps of tangled stems may be as little as six inches tall, hugging the sandy hummocks and stabilizing them. Under better conditions it may grow to five feet and be tree-shaped.

The slender, cylindrical, gray-green stems are less that a half-inch in diameter. The entire surface is closely set with flattened, diamond-shaped or obovate tubercles with only a thin groove etched between them. The areole is a notch or groove at the upper end of the tubercle.

Tan-sheathed central spines an inch to three inches long begin to develop in the uppermost areoles. Ultimately, all but one of these abort, leaving a single spine, an inch and a half to two and three-quarters inches long. Each spine is robust and strongly barbed.

Flowering takes place from May to September, in the shimmering heat of summer. The flowers, a half-inch in diameter, develop on the upper areoles of short lateral branches. Petal color varies from bronzy to orangy yellow. The fruit is dry, densely spiny and burr-like and, at a half-inch wide and three-quarters of an inch long, relatively large. Spines on the fruit may be up to three-quarters of an inch long. The plants are relatively slow-growing, even in cultivation.

Diamond Cholla   Cactaceae   *Opuntia ramosissima*

Buckhorn Cholla

Buckhorn Cholla is a common shrubby or tree-like cactus of California, Nevada, Utah and western and southern Arizona. The species has four generally recognized varieties. Extensive stands may be found from a few hundred feet above sea level to the 3,500-foot level.

The cylindrical branches are attached at such angles that the structure suggests the antlers of the diminutive desert deer. Typical joints are six to twenty-four inches long and are covered in conspicuous elongated tubercles. Each tubercle is beset with a cluster of overlapping reddish to tannish-white spines. Sheaths are evident on newer spines; after a year or so, the sheaths weather away and the spines turn first brown, then black.

Red, purplish or yellow flowers appear in the spring at the tips of branches. The spiny fruit which follows is dry at maturity. The buds are still collected in the spring by traditional Tohono O'odham, who toss them in gravelly sand and brush them with homemade brooms to remove the spines. Dried and later steamed, the buds provide a nutritious and very tasty vegetable with a texture, aroma and taste that whispers of asparagus.

Buckhorn Cholla   Cactaceae   *Opuntia acanthocarpa*

Beavertail Cactus

Prickly pears have flattened, jointed stems. They take many different shapes; the Beavertail cactus has joints shaped like a beaver's tail. It is a low-growing, clustering species of the desert areas of the western half of Arizona and adjacent areas of California and Utah.

The prickly pears form a large group within the cactus family. They and the chollas differ from other Southwestern cacti in that their areoles bear tiny, easily-dislodged barbed spines called glochids. The glochids are densely clustered in the dimple-like depressions of the areoles, which are scattered uniformly across the surface of the velvety blue-gray stems. Otherwise, except for one of the four Arizona varieties, the prickly pears bear no spines.

This cacti is one of the earliest to bloom. Following a warm winter, the magenta, yellow or occasionally white flowers appear as early as late February. Like all prickly pears, flowering normally occurs from the areoles on the margins of the upper half of the joint.

When ripe, the fruit is dry and inedible, and useless for the making of traditional prickly pear jelly. Nor are the stems edible as *nopalitos,* the diced cactus stems served as a vegetable in the Southwest. At one time the stems were used as medicine in the treatment of syphilis among indigenous peoples. The plant is easily and commonly cultivated in its native range.

Beavertail Cactus   Cactaceae   *Opuntia basilaris*

Golden-flowered Century Plant

Century plants, also known as *maguey* or *mescal,* are another large group which, because of their long and close association with mankind, have fostered many legends and beliefs. Foremost among these folktales is that agaves live for a hundred years before flowering and dying.

Agaves store food and moisture in their succulent stems and leaves and especially in the leaf bases. In some species, this storing process may continue up to forty years; for other species the time may be as short as seven years. At the end of this building period each plant suddenly, over a period of a few weeks or months, thrusts up a spike or huge branching pyramidal inflorescence bearing robust clusters of flowers.

In Arizona alone there are fourteen native kinds of century plants. They range from dwarf species only six inches in diameter to massive plants four feet wide and equally high. All are characterized by having dagger-like leaves arranged in rosettes. The leaves may be broad or narrow and toothed or toothless.

The intense chrome-yellow flowers of the Golden-flowered Century Plant make it unique. The flower stalk may be up to twenty feet high with eight to eighteen branches, restricted to the uppermost third or quarter of the stalk. This agave is found only in central Arizona; the center of its range is the region around the town of Superior. The flowering plant draws nocturnal flocks of nectar-feeding bats to pollinate it as well as the attention of even the most casual human passerby.

Clinging to steep rocky slopes, cliffs and outcrops at elevations between 3,000 and 6,000 feet, this agave grows with cacti and other succulents and even with junipers and oaks at the highest elevations of its range.

Mature rosettes are up to four feet across and have few of the small plants, called offsets, that form around the bases of mother plants. The leaves are eighteen inches to two feet long and shaped like lance heads. They are ashy-gray with the edges turned up to form a trough. Each leaf is fiercely armed, bristling along the margins with dagger-shaped flattened teeth that are brownish-gray, a quarter-inch to half-inch long. The teeth may be straight or bent. In addition, each leaf is tipped with a brown or gray, conical, grooved spine an inch and a half long. The spine is capable of inflicting a severe puncture wound.

Indian groups of the Southwest and Mesoamerica found many uses for century plants. To prepare them as food, the nearly mature rosettes were harvested and the leaves cut back to the bases. The heads, which then looked like pineapples, were hauled to a central location.

Golden-flowered Century Plant   Agavaceae   *Agave chrysantha*

The Indians dug a large pit and lined it with rocks, filled it with fuel and started a fire. When the fire burned down, green plant material was layered over the coals and ashes, followed by the harvested century plants and then another layer of vegetation. Over everything went a thick blanket of soil. Two to four days later the agave was unearthed and eaten on the spot or pounded in a rock mortar, in which case the resulting pulpy-fibrous mass was formed into cakes and dried for later use.

The taste is similar to that of molasses. Many Indian groups not living near sources of mescal made long annual trips to secure a supply of this sweet. After chewing and sucking out the juice and pulp, they spat out the residue; the expectorated fibrous masses are called quids and are an abundant feature of well-preserved archaeological sites in agave country. The Mescalero Apaches of southern New Mexico derive their name from this practice, a *mescalero* being a person who harvests and prepares mescal.

Agaves lend themselves to a number of uses. Fibers such as *sisal, henequen* and *ixtle* are still commercially produced from the leaves of Mexican species. The fiber is made into twine, rope, netting, cloth, baskets, brushes and other useful objects. Medicinal chemicals are a by-product of the cordage industry. The Apaches even made a one-stringed violin from the hollowed-out flower stalk. Flower stalks and dried leaves are still sometimes used in rural Mexico to build rude shelters in fields and even permanent housing.

Mexican century plants also provide various alcoholic beverages. Traditionally, plants were harvested from the wild or from small cultivated plots or hedgerows. The fermented juice is called *pulque* and is drunk fresh or used in flavoring baked goods. When the roasted heads are mashed, fermented and distilled, the product is known as *mescal.* This product is frequently made and consumed locally or regionally, although a few areas with cottage-industry distillers have achieved national reputations because of the quality of their illicit spirits. Most notable of these is *Bacanora,* made in the general vicinity of Rancho Bacanora in eastern Sonora. Most famous of all the mescals, of course, are the *tequilas* from west-central Mexico. There, vast plantations of blue *Agave tequilana* support large-scale, legal production of Mexico's most famous indigenous liquor.

Flowers of the Century Plant

Sotol or Desert Spoon

Sotol grows as a rosette of many strap-like leaves closely set on their margins with vicious flattened triangular teeth. Short-stemmed or stemless, the clumps grow to five feet wide.

The leaves are two to three feet long, blue-green or lime-green and brushy at the tips. Tan at the base, the teeth turn brown at the tips and sometimes bend in various directions to make passage near the clumps even more difficult.

A single inflorescence develops from the apex of the clump. It may be up to fifteen feet high and was used at one time as the shaft for Indian lances. Usually the flowers on a given inflorescence are all staminate or all pistillate, but a few flowers of the opposite sex are occasionally mixed in. The inflorescence is narrow, generally more so in mature male plants than in mature, fruiting, female plants.

Flowers are borne in linear clusters, two to four inches long, on side branches on the flower stalk. Flowers are about three-eighths of an inch wide, with six petals enclosing six stamens or one stout pistil. The fruit is a single-seeded, three-winged capsule, three-eighths of an inch long and notched at the apex.

The shiny brown or tan leaf bases from dead plants resemble spoons; hence the common name. The base dries in a broad concave curve, with the leaf itself forming the handle of the spoon. The leaves have been used in modern and ancient basketry and plaiting work in the Southwest. In Mexico, the leafless stems, *cabezas,* are roasted in pits, mashed and fermented. The product is distilled into a fiery clear or amber liquor called *sotol.*

Sotol or Desert Spoon   Agavaceae   *Dasylirion wheeleri*

Arizona Rainbow Cactus

One of Arizona's and New Mexico's most spectacular flowering cacti, *Echinocereus pectinatus* var. *rigidissimus* is a member of the hedgehog cactus group. Unlike many of the common clumping hedgehogs, it is usually a single robust stem, from two and a half to four inches in diameter. Occasionally, the plants are sparingly branched. Individual plants may be up to fifteen inches tall.

The radial spines are closely and uniformly set on elliptical areoles, overlapping adjacent spines and completely obscuring the pale green stem. This is especially true under drought conditions, when the stems contract. Alternating between reddish-pink and tan, the spines form horizontal color bands that give the plants a striped or rainbow pattern. There are no central spines in this variety, and the radials are often flattened against the plant body so that the plants are comparatively safe and easy to handle.

The flowers give this already intriguing plant a truly spectacular appearance in June and August. The flowers are rose-magenta wheels two and a half to four inches in diameter, with white or yellowish centers. A plant with two or three open flowers is completely obscured beneath a festive parasol.

As is typical of hedgehog cacti, the fruit is a spherical berry which turns tomato-red and sloughs off its spines at maturity. The fruit is edible; the pulp is reddish and juicy, but with many tiny black seeds imbedded in it.

Arizona Rainbow Cactus   Cactaceae   *Echinocereus pectinatus* var. *rigidissimus*

Pencil Cholla

This cholla is a very handsome shrub, densely and intricately branched. Because it frequently develops a robust trunk it sometimes looks like a dwarf tree.

It is easy to see how the plant got its name: the branches are slender, being less than a half-inch in diameter, with very reduced tubercles on joints two inches to six inches long.

One to four spines per areole is normal. They are reddish-tan with loose-fitting sheaths. The largest spine, usually down-turned, is a half-inch to an inch and three-quarters long and flattened at the base.

The flowers are uninspiring green, yellow or muddy-orange, three-quarters of an inch wide. The fleshy fruit is short and conical; sterile fruit is elongated. The fruit is green, suffused with purple on the low tubercles. Usually the fruits are without spines, but young fruit may have a few robust glochids. The boiled stems were eaten by desert Indians, particularly when other food was scarce.

Pencil Cholla   Cactaceae   *Opuntia arbuscula*

Flame Flower

In addition to being one of the most common of Southwestern wildflowers, *Talinum auriantiacum* is a succulent. Each winter the plant freezes to the ground; with the onset of the summer rains, the perennial tuberous root sprouts again. It is often abundant in desert grasslands, plains and rocky slopes from western Texas to southern Arizona and northern Mexico, at elevations between 4,000 feet and 5,000 feet.

The flowers are orange, have five petals and are three-quarters of an inch wide. Two to five flowers bloom in clusters from leaf axils. For talinums, the flowers are large and showy.

A few stout, succulent stems fifteen inches tall bear alternate, fleshy leaves, linear to lanceolate in shape. Each leaf bears a single prominent midvein.

Flame Flower   Portulacaceae   *Talinum auriantiacum*

Sea Purslane

We almost always assume that succulent plants are perennial. But such is not always the case; though it can persist through the winter if protected from frost, Sea Purslane is usually regarded as an annual. It is native from Kansas to central California south into the American tropics.

Sesuvium verrucosum is a prostrate herb with coarse succulent stems and fleshy leaves with smooth margins. Leaves have pointed or rounded tips and taper gradually toward a base that slightly clasps the stem.

Sea Purslane flowers from March to November. The flowers lack petals, although the peculiar sepals serve the function. The sepals are green on the outside and prolonged into a pointed tip. Inside, the sepals are fleshy and white, flushed with rose or orange. As the sepals open, the cluster of numerous rosy stamens is revealed. The whole flower is only a half-inch wide.

Sesuvium occasionally shows up at specialty arid-land plant sales in the Southwest. It is used as a ground cover in frost-free areas or as a hanging-basket patio plant.

Sea Purslane   Aizoaceae   *Sesuvium verrucosum*

Desert Hen-and-Chicks

With less of the whitish, waxy powder covering its leaves, the Arizona subspecies of *Dudleya pulverulenta* differs from the typical California coastal subspecies of the same species name. It is a plant of very arid mountain ranges of western Arizona, southern Nevada, southern California and Baja California del Norte. Rocky slopes and crevices between 500 feet and 2,500 feet are its commonest habitat.

The appearance changes dramatically with the seasons. In the dry season there may be as few as ten very short leaves, essentially maintaining only the center of a normal rosette. In the wet winter and spring there may be as many as sixty robust leaves, six and a half inches long. The rosettes may be single or clustered; in either case they form at the tips of branches. Usually the prostrate stems are covered by the organic remains of dried leaves.

April to August is the normal bloom period. The pink succulent inflorescence has thick clasping bracts; the flowers it carries nod prior to opening. The five clear-yellow or red petals are fused into a tube for more than half their length.

Despite its desert habitat, cultivating this species requires careful attention to watering. The plants grow quickly and lushly during warm, moist winters, but direct overhead watering during hot dry weather can lead to the death of the plant due to bacterial attack.

Desert Hen-and-Chicks   Crassulaceae   *Dudleya pulverulenta* spp. *arizonica*

Rusby's Hen-and-Chicks

Graptopetalum rusbyi has been passed back and forth between the genus *Echeverria* and *Graptopetalum*. The argument rages from generation to generation between botanists and need concern no one but the belligerents.

Plants of this species are tiny; flowering plants may be only an inch across and as high. Appearing in April and May, the flowers are pale yellow and mottled with purple-red.

Several of the lead-colored rosettes may perch in a shallow pock-mark on a basalt cliff face in a shady canyon. That is the typical habitat, although occasionally robust colonies may be found in deeper, moister soils. Then the giants among the species appear, with individual rosettes as much as two and a half inches across.

Rusby's Hen-and-Chicks is found only in central Arizona. Despite its delicate beauty and relative ease of cultivation, the plant is little-known; its habitat is mostly inaccessible except to the cliff-grappler and avid hiker, and the few roads that enter its domain are narrow and twisted.

Rusby's Hen-and-Chicks   Crassulaceae   *Graptopetalum rusbyi*

Wildflowers

The word *wildflower* evokes the freshness and renewal of spring. It suggests shady forest grottoes, sodden mountain meadows alive with the sounds of insects and birds, and prairies burning with color. Wildflowers announce that winter has gone, that spring and summer have risen anew.

The arid regions of the southwestern United States receive these joyous outpourings in full but sporadic measure. A decade may pass between the truly magnificient displays; bulbs, seeds, tubers, rhizomes and perennials with annual above-ground portions may wait long months or years between periods of rainfall sufficient to support a reproductive cycle. In between these awesome times, scattered local displays may add to the soil's storehouse of seed.

The region experiences two rainfall seasons each year, separated by a prolonged period of drought. Summers are scorching; air temperatures shoot past the hundred-degree mark every day. But if winter rains begin in late September or in October, when the night temperatures are still relatively warm; and if sufficient rain falls again at intervals of two to four weeks, with warming periods in between; and if the winter has light or no frost; and if this pattern continues into the middle of spring, then the desert will become a sea, flooded with hundreds of different kinds of annuals and perennials in full flower. Because the equation is so complex, such a display is rare. Spectacular years are long-remembered; two were 1941 and 1974.

Winter rains are usually brought by wide storm-fronts, moving across large areas. By mid-May, desert winds and climbing temperatures have left the earth bereft of moisture, and the shallow-rooted annuals have already withered. They leave behind dried, highly combustible remains and millions of seeds to await the next cycle of growth.

Summer rains are different in character, spawned by thunderstorms which build up in the midafternoon as the land heats up. The clouds rise and cool, causing the water vapor they carry to condense and fall in great cloudbursts over localized areas. This brings about very scattered displays of wildflowers. Up to half the total yearly rainfall may fall within a few hours and commonly results in flash flooding of short duration.

Traditionally, the summer rains start on San Juan's Day, June 24. This is the approximate time of the summer solstice and the time when the Tohono O'odham and other desert Indians plant unirrigated summer crops. The crops have adapted to much the same growing conditions as the summer wildflowers and in some cases are domesticated relatives of wildlings. Amaranths and sunflowers fall into this category.

Desert wildflowers are not adapted, in the usual sense of the word, to the heat of summer, when ground surface temperatures may reach 170 degrees F. Although they make efficient use of the available moisture, many species simply avoid the heat and dryness by germinating, flowering and disseminating seeds in a single wet season. The seed is buried by wind-blown soil or sifts down into the cooler, higher-humidity space between gravel particles, is eaten by animals, or is buried by soil moved down slopes by water.

Many of the plants are tuberous, tuberous-rooted, rhizomatous or shrubby perennials, which spend their winters and summers below ground or in a dessicated state. If rainfall permits and warm night-time temperatures continue, some species may continue flowering well into the fall, even though extended periods of hundred-degree temperatures are sometimes experienced in September and even October. Displays can be spectacular, but never with the diversity of species offered in exceptional spring shows.

Even the winter season has a few adapted species. Chuparosa (Hummingbird Bush, *Justicia californica*) and Brittle Bush (*Encelia californica*) are two which commonly flower in January and February.

Sometimes no water is better than some water; light rains might stimulate germination without providing sufficient moisture to sustain the plant through its reproductive cycle. Some seeds contain chemical inhibitors which prevent germination during light rains. The seeds of many desert plants, such as the palo verdes (*Cercidium* spp.) and the mesquites (*Prosopis* spp.), have very hard seed coats. For the seeds to germinate, the impermeable coats must be worn away through the action of soil chemicals, by passing through the gut of wild or domestic animals, or by tumbling through the sand and gravel. When this is done, water from the next substantial downpour can be absorbed by the seed. If temperatures are right for that particular species, then germination can proceed.

The best shows come after winters of heavy and uniform rainfall, but every year produces wildflowers. Even when scanty rain dictates a "no show" season, the diligent searcher should be rewarded; it just takes more work. The best places to look are in desert canyons and arroyo banks, among the rocks and boulders on north and east slopes and in the protective canopy of trees and shrubs. These microhabitats receive less solar radiation and more protection from winds, so the soil does not dry out as fast as in open or exposed areas.

Some wildflowers are "belly flowers," so named because they are so short or have such small flowers that to fully appreciate them, the observer is forced to ground level. No desert flower enthusiast would approach a vacant city lot without a jeweler's loupe or similar lens close at hand.

Whether an uncultivated plant is a weed or a wildflower is largely a matter of the circumstances of its growth. Many plants, both native and naturalized, grow readily on disturbed soils such as gardens, ditch banks, agricultural fields, road margins and newly seeded lawns. In such situations, most people would classify fiddleneck (*Amsinckia* spp.) and London Rocket (*Sisymbrium irio*) as weeds. But few people have trouble juggling them and many other species into the category of wildflower when the plants are mixed with others in a natural setting, on wash banks and at the shady sides of shrubs and trees. The reclassification takes place even though the observer cursed them the past weekend while wrenching them from among the beans and onions. Thus the old definition of a weed as "a plant out of place" seems apt.

Many perennial wildflowers are protected by strict laws, strictly enforced. Often, seeds may be taken only with the permission of the landowner or authority having jurisdiction over the land. Much of the land in the Southwest is public, administered by the Forest Service, Bureau of Land Management, military departments and other county, state and federal agencies. Indian reservations also account for large tracts.

Wildflower Growth Regions

	Arizona	California	Colorado	Nevada	New Mexico	Texas	Utah
Desert Chicory	■	■		■	■	■	■
Ajo Lily	■	■		■			■
Desert Bluebonnet	■	■		■			■
Desert Mariposa	■	■		■	■		■
Parry Beardtongue	■						
Chuparosa	■	■					
Desert Larkspur	■			■	■		■
Gordon's Bladderpod	■	■		■	■	■	
Desert Tobacco	■	■	■	■	■	■	■
Heron's-bill	■	■	■		■	■	
Sand Verbena	■	■					
Twist-flower	■						
Bluestem Pricklepoppy	■	■	■		■		■
Desert Marigold	■	■	■	■	■	■	■
Fleabane	■	■		■	■	■	
Blue Flax	■	■		■	■	■	
Coulter's Hibiscus	■					■	
Purple Groundcherry	■						
Southwestern Ruellia	■						
Saiya	■						
Dune Evening Primrose	■	■			■		
Purple Mat	■	■			■	■	■
Desert Zinnia	■				■	■	
Fairy Duster	■	■			■		
Magenta Four O'Clock	■	■	■		■	■	■

Desert Chicory

The flowers of Desert Chicory very much resemble chicory, a widespread weed introduced from Europe. The two are closely related, being placed in the same sub-family of the Compositae, the Sunflower family. However, the petals of our desert native are white, flushed with pink or purple. The European petals are pure blue. Desert Chicory's habitats are the plains and mesas of the Southwest below 3,000 feet; in the desert it is often abundant.

The delicate puffs of fruiting flower heads are quite conspicuous as they ripen. The fruits are like dandelions; they drift on the wind until they lodge among the tangled stems and leaves of desert shrubs. Sifting through the branches, the fruits lose their umbrella-like parachutes of feathery down as they fall to the moist, shady soil below.

Germination follows winter rains, with the weak blue-gray stems supported in the branches of the sheltering plant. The blossoms are an inch to an inch and a half wide and consist of many single flowers united in a single head, a characteristic typical of the family. The individual flowers have strap-shaped five-toothed corollas.

The leaves are sparse, alternately arranged, with their bases partially circling the stems. The leaves are similar in shape to dandelion leaves, but coarser, with slightly prickly margins.

Desert Chicory is easy to start from seed and grows twenty to thirty inches tall. In the Southwest, sow in the fall and enjoy the long-flowering annual from February to July. The genus name is derived from Constantin Samuel Rafinesque, an eccentric botanist of the late eighteenth and early nineteenth centuries. The first specimens were presumably found in New Mexico, hence the species name.

Desert Chicory   Compositae   *Rafinesquia neomexicana*

Ajo Lily

Among the most remarkable of the desert wildflowers, Ajo Lilies grow in the driest, hottest portion of southwestern Arizona and northern Mexico, on sand dunes and plains covered with creosote bushes. They are members of the Lily family; the fragrant flowers look like small versions of commercial Easter lilies.

The flowers are two inches to three inches long, with three petals and three petal-like sepals. They are satiny white with green stripes and glisten in the shimmering heat. Several years may lapse between flowerings; in the interim years, only the leaves make an occasional appearance above ground.

Flowering stalks emerge from rosettes of two to six gracefully curved leaves. The leaves are six inches to twelve inches long, with deep channels and wavy edges. As the leaf tips move back and forth in the wind, they trace arcs in the sandy soil.

Leaves and stalks arise from a bulb buried six inches to two feet deep. Descending even deeper, the roots are a cluster of fragile, sand-encrusted succulent rods about ten inches long. Brown papery scales cover the bulb, which is one to two inches in diameter. When the bulbs go dormant at the end of the growing season, even the roots dry up and die to conserve moisture.

Flowering is in March and April; left behind are dry leafless stalks that bear squat capsules an inch in diameter. The pods split open to allow the wind to lift and distribute the thin shiny black seeds.

The bulbs are edible, although slimy, starchy and protected by law. *Ajo* is Spanish for garlic, which the bulbs superficially resemble. The plants are abundant in the vicinity of Ajo, a copper-mining town in the parched lands west of Tucson, and may have lent it their name.

Despite its beauty and desirability, widespread cultivation of this plant is unlikely. It is four years from seed to first flowering, and the bulbs rot if allowed to remain wet in the summer heat.

Ajo Lily   Liliaceae   *Hesperocallis undulata*

Desert Bluebonnet

Despite the specific part of the scientific name, which means few or sparsely flowered, Desert Bluebonnet is one of the desert's most prolific and showy annuals. After exceptional winter rains, whole mountainsides at elevations below 4,500 feet may be flooded in a sky-blue cascade. Even in years of moderate rainfall, runoff produces roadside stands over a foot tall at intermediate elevations.

Desert Bluebonnets are typical of the pea and bean subfamily of the Leguminosae; the flowers, a half-inch long, resemble those of sweet peas. They are arranged in elongate, leafless clusters at the tips of branches.

Leaves and stems are covered with fine, silvery hairs. Divided into five to seven finger-like linear lobes, the leaves are attached to the stems by flattened stalks an inch to three inches long. The leaves alternate on the stem and become progressively smaller near the flower cluster.

The bean-like fruit is slightly indented around each spotted gray seed. As the inch-long pods ripen they pop open suddenly, catapulting the seed some distance. The two halves of the pod remain behind, each in a tight twisted spiral. Alkaloid chemicals make the seeds extremely poisonous, especially to sheep.

Perfect drainage and full sun are necessary to grow this lupine; gravelly soil is best. Otherwise, they are not fussy about their needs. Sown in fall and kept moist until well up, they amply repay the investment in time and water.

Desert Bluebonnet   Leguminosae   *Lupinus sparsiflorus*

Desert Mariposa

The first sighting of this stunning plant is one of the great moments for any wildflower lover. A brilliant flame-orange or clear intense-yellow beacon, Desert Mariposa can be found among other annuals and grasses in April, May and June. It grows throughout the Southwest on rocky or gravelly slopes and mesas below 5,000 feet.

Three broad, rounded petals form a chalice two inches or more across. At the base of each petal is a dark brown or black spot with a raised, broad gland and a scattering of robust orange-black hairs. The sepals are slender, green and pointed, with whitish margins. Six equal stamens bear purple anthers and filaments. Two or three flowers cluster on stems that are two inches to eighteen inches long.

Individual flowers shed their pollen before their stigmata are developed sufficiently to receive it. This prevents self-pollination and increases the genetic diversity of the population by enforcing out-crossing.

But for the flowers, the plant would make no impression. The leaves are sparse and grass-like, clasping the stem beneath the flower cluster. The leaves are deeply channeled, curved and covered with a waxy gray coating. There are one to three branches at most.

The fruit is a tan capsule, three inches long with brown vertical stripes. The capsule is triangular in cross section, tapering at both ends. It splits open on drying to reveal three neat stacks of tan wafer-like seeds.

The Mariposa Lily has an edible bulb an inch in diameter. Propogation is from seed sown in the fall in pots or protected beds; flowering can be expected in the fourth or fifth year. They are difficult to keep alive because the bulbs tend to rot if over-watered, especially in the heat of the summer.

Desert Mariposa   Liliaceae   *Calochortus kennedyi*

Parry Beardtongue

Of Arizona's forty-plus species and varieties of *Penstemon,* Parry Beardtongue is the most desert-adapted. It is also found in Sonora, Mexico, at elevations between 1,500 feet and 5,000 feet. The plant is a member of the large Figwort family.

As are most penstemons, it is a perennial herb, sending up between one and twenty-five or more unbranched stems like wands from the base of the tough root-crown. The stems are erect or ascending, and up to four feet tall.

Flowers are hot pink to rose-magenta and restricted to the upper two-thirds of the stems. The five petals are fused into an inflated tube except at the tips, which form rounded lobes. The three lower lobes are larger than the two upper ones. There are five stamens: two long ones that curve and arch into the top of the open throat of the flower; two shorter ones in the bottom-rear of the corolla; and one long, sterile, hairy one on the floor of the corolla. This last one gives the group its distinctive common name.

Depending on the availability of shade and moisture, the leaves are dark green to ashy gray with a bloom like a grape. Leaves are opposite, with smooth margins. The lower leaves are broad, blunt at the tips and narrowed at the base. They are up to an inch wide and six inches long, though usually smaller. As they near the flowers the leaves become narrower, more pointed and lance-shaped.

Never abundant, the plants occupy a wide variety of habitats including arroyo banks, road margins, rocky hillsides and narrow canyons. One of the very few native perennial herbs available in local nurseries, they self-seed and reproduce freely in home gardens with minimum care.

Parry Beardtongue   Scrophulariaceae   *Penstemon parryi*

Chuparosa or Hummingbird Bush

This drought-hardy twiggy gray shrub provides abundant, brilliant color during the fall and winter, when little else is in flower. Severe frost may kill the branches back to the ground in the northern part of its range, but it quickly recovers and resumes flowering. Making its home in gravel washes and rocky hillsides in southwestern Arizona, southeastern California and northwest Mexico, the plant grows to six feet tall.

The tubular corollas are orange-red, two-lipped, to two inches long, forming in clusters at the tips of the branches. Tasting somewhat like a hairy cucumber, the flowers were formerly eaten by the Tohono O'odham. The sweet nectar was considered a delicacy; pressed out of the bottom of the flower tube and allowed to harden, it is similar to rock candy. The plants also provide some browse for cattle.

Leaves range in shape from ovate to rounded-triangular or triangular and fall off during the summer. The entire surface of the plant is covered with microscopic flat white hairs which reflect the intense sunlight. This is a common feature of desert plants worldwide.

Seed is difficult to obtain because, as with many members of the Acanthus family, it is formed in a four-seeded capsule which explodes on drying. This sends the seeds flying in every direction.

Until recently the plant has seen little horticultural use. It is easily propogated from cuttings rooted in damp sand with bottom heat. When it starts looking a little shabby, the brittle stems may be broken off close to the ground; the plants quickly regenerate them in a uniform mound.

Chuparosa or Hummingbird Bush   Acanthaceae   *Justicia californica*

Desert Larkspur

Yellows and whites predominate among desert wildflowers; the most striking feature of this widespread perennial is the phenomenally intense color in its royal blue flowers.

Between March and June, stalks sprout from compact rosettes of broad gray-green lobed leaves. The slender stalks are two and a half to three feet tall and nearly leafless. Spiraling around the upper half of the stalks are three to twelve flowers, three-quarters of an inch to an inch and a quarter long. The plants tend to occur in colonies on rocky slopes and gravelly mesas, but sometimes crop up in the open desert.

The fruit is a papery capsule with three parts. The seeds inside look like poppy seeds; the capsule splits down the inside and, vibrating in the wind, disperses the seeds over the nearby ground.

Although larkspurs and many other species of the Ranunculus family are poisonous to various classes of livestock, the Hopi Indians use the plant as a ritual emetic and grind the dried flowers with cornmeal to make "blue pollen" for the Flute Clan altars during kiva ceremonies.

Propogation is by seed sown in the fall in protected locations on gravelly soil with good drainage. The leaves and stalks wither to the ground in the summer, only to sprout again in the fall. Gardeners therefore must be careful not to cultivate the soil in areas where the buried root-crowns are resting.

Desert Larkspur   Ranunculaceae   *Delphinium scaposum*

Gordon's Bladderpod

Virtually the entire Southwest below 5,000 feet is home to Gordon's Bladderpod. In Arizona alone there are nine species of bladderpod; this winter-spring annual herb is the most common and characteristic.

The flowers are typical of the mustards: bright yellow, three-eights of an inch wide, with four petals and four sepals. Of the six stamens, two are short and four are long.

Even in the driest years a few poorly developed individuals can always be found from February to May. In wet years, extensive stands carpet desert and plain in huge patches, filling in the normally bare area between creosote bushes (*Larrea*) and bursage (*Ambrosia* spp.) with the cumulative effect of their blossoms.

The plant is semi-erect, branching near the base. White hairs with five or six branches cover the slender stems and leaves. Including the stalk, lower leaves are up to two inches long and may bear a few teeth or be divided into lobes. Those further up are usually without stalks and teeth. All are very narrowly elliptic in outline and alternate on the stem.

The fruit, the source of the common name, is a spherical inflated pod an eighth-inch in diameter, containing about ten tiny seeds. The dried style forms an attached beak. An edible oil had been expressed from the seeds experimentally, but no commercial use has followed.

As with most desert annuals, fall sowing and persistent watering until established is all that is needed to effect a showy stand.

Gordon's Bladderpod   Cruciferae   *Lesquerella gordoni*

Desert Tobacco

Found in sandy and gravelly soils throughout the Southwest, Desert Tobacco is an annual or perennial herb up to four feet tall, covered with sticky glandular hairs.

The inch-long tubular flowers are greenish white, with the stamens fused to the petal tube for about a quarter of the distance up from the base. Flaring at the lip, the tube has five blunt points or lobes. The five sepal lobes are very pointed and close tightly about the petal tube. At lower elevations the plants flower year-round.

The leaves are medium green, an inch and a half to two inches wide and up to six inches long. Lower leaves have winged stalks; upper leaves are smaller and often lack stalks. They are more or less lance-shaped or broadest toward the pointed tip. If broadest at the base, the leaf usually partially clasps the stem. The leaves are alternately arranged and give off a distinctive odor when crushed.

To newcomers, Desert Tobacco is a weed. But among Hopi, Tohono O'odham and Navajo traditionalists, reverence for the plant is universal. At Niman Kachina, a Hopi ceremony given to honor and thank departing helpful spirits, the kachinas or spirits are blessed by priests who blow clouds of smoke on them as they go. The smoke represents clouds, which in turn represent rain. The plant is also used in curing rites, and magic powers are attributed to it.

The leaves, stems and flowers contain nicotine, a well-known alkaloid, and are poisonous to livestock and humans. Since the lethal dose is about two percent of body weight, ingestion is not a serious hazard to humans.

Seed capsules are brown, three-eighths of an inch long. The seeds are minute, smaller than a pin-head, and may be collected all year. An easy plant to grow, it can be sown at any time of the year and kept moist until established.

Desert Tobacco   Solanaceae   *Nicotiana trigonophylla*

Heron's-bill

A common winter-spring annual, Heron's-bill is related to the geraniums and is placed in that family. It is a plant of open deserts, mesas and desert pavement areas. In dry years it hugs the ground and may be only a few inches across; in wet winters and springs it may be up to three feet wide and ten inches tall.

Clusters of three to five flowers appear on short stalks that originate from the axils of the leaves near the stem tips. The five separate petals are magenta and form a shallow cup up to a half-inch wide.

The plants branch at the base, forming irregular rosettes. The leaves are ovate to roughly triangular, heart-shaped at the base, with deep or shallow lobes. Leaf blades are an inch long and densely covered with very short hairs, pressed flat. The leaf stalks are slender and up to two inches long.

The maturing fruit looks like an erect, slender heron's bill. As it dries, the five parts of the maturing ovulary separate, each of the divisions pulling a strip of the long, narrow style column with it. As drying continues, the strips twist into tight spirals, like corkscrews. When the fruits are moistened again the strips slowly untwist; under favorable soil conditions this augers the seeds into the ground, a very convenient self-planting mechanism. Seeds are dispersed by wind, animal fur and human stockings, and hours can be spent gleaning them from knit clothing.

Heron's-bill   Geraniaceae   *Erodium texanum*

Sand Verbena

Members of the Four O'Clock family, six recognized species of *Abronia* grow in the southwestern third of Arizona and in adjoining areas of California and the Mexican state of Sonora. Of these, the most common and spectacular displays are made by *Abronia villosa*. After unusually wet winters, millions of blossoms paint the landscape; during the spring of 1974, an area forty miles northeast of Yuma was purple from horizon to horizon.

Clusters of five to fifteen flowers form hemispherical heads up to two inches wide, held erect on slender stalks from the axils of the leaves. Whether the plant is annual or perennial depends on growing conditions, though in nature the above-ground portions of the plant dry up and blow away as summer approaches.

The plants form mounds up to three feet in diameter which dot the sandy plains below 1,500 feet. The stems trail along the surface and bear opposite, ovate leaves from swollen nodules. The leaves are three-fourths of an inch to two inches long and have smooth margins. All above-ground parts of the plant are covered by short sticky hairs.

The fruits are broad-winged papery affairs, suitable for wind distribution. This papery calyx should be removed by hand before sowing the seeds. If the plant is to be grown within its native range, the seed may be broadcast on the open ground and raked in lightly. The soil should be sandy, loose and fine-textured, and watering should be thorough and frequent enough to insure that the seedlings do not dry out.

Sand Verbena   Nyctaginaceae   *Abronia villosa*

Twist-flower

This common annual is a conspicuous member of the Mustard family. It is strictly erect, to twenty-five inches tall, with a few ascending branches. It is usually found at elevations between 1,500 and 4,500 feet, growing in colonies on rocky or gravelly slopes among desert trees and shrubs and along the banks of arroyos.

The typical variety has ivory flowers with purple-brown veins, three-eighths of an inch to a half-inch long. The flowers are shaped like urns, with the four individual petals sticking out of the neck of the tightly enclosing petal-like sepals. Curling back, the petals almost touch the sepals. A rare variety, known only from Diablo Canyon in the Organ Pipe Cactus National Monument, is bright yellow with a wide, satiny, purple-brown stripe down each petal.

Stems and leaves have a bluish-purple cast and a waxy bloom similar to a grape. The plants are without hairs or glands on the foliage, and flowers and leaves are alternate on the stems. The leaves vary in shape, but are mostly lance-shaped, with a few prickles on the margins. Becoming sparser and smaller toward the top of the plant, the leaves are from an inch and a half to ten inches long.

The fruits are flat, smooth pods held strictly erect and parallel to the stems. As in all mustards, a translucent partition runs the length of the pod, separating the two lines of seeds. Seeds are broad and flat and bear a papery wing at the margin. Fruits are robust, a quarter of an inch wide and up to three inches long.

Twist-flowers are easy to cultivate within their native range. Seed should be broadcast in the fall on gravelly soil, raked in lightly and kept moist until the seedlings are well established. Thereafter, an occasional thorough soaking, when dry, will suffice.

Twist-flower   Cruciferae   *Streptanthus arizonicus*

Bluestem Pricklepoppy

This blue-green perennial herb is hard to miss. It stands two to four feet tall, wears a dense coat of spines and bears clusters of flowers that look like fried eggs. The plant blooms throughout the summer, from the western Great Plains and Rocky Mountains south to Mexico and west into Arizona and California. A pioneer plant which invades when potential competitors have been removed, it is common in disturbed soil along roads and in over-grazed fields.

The flowers are three inches wide, with four to six white petals and a cluster of yellow-orange stamens at the center. Hence the vernacular: Fried-Egg Plant. The flowers tremble in the slightest breeze, frustrating every attempt to photograph them.

This plant rarely makes its way into floral arrangements or the alimentary tracts of grazing animals, since needly spines cover every above-ground part except the flowers. A true poppy, the seeds and oils contained in the plants include poisonous alkaloids which cause vomiting, diarrhea, hallucinations and coma. Ingestion usually happens when the seeds are harvested in grain fields where it is a weed. The juice of related species has been used in the treatment of skin disease.

Bluestem Pricklepoppy   **Papaveraceae**   *Argemone pleiacantha*

Desert Marigold

Desert Marigold is a common perennial on gravelly soils in open desert; along roads, it frequently forms nearly pure stands, crowding the pavement like a formal border. It is found in disturbed soil from sea level to 5,000 feet, from Texas to California and from Utah to northern Mexico.

The grayish, wand-like stems are eighteen inches high above rosettes of wooly gray leaves. Each stem carries a single head of two different types of flowers arranged in a disc an inch to an inch and three-quarters wide. Like many of the members of the Compositae or Sunflower family, Desert Marigold has several series of flat, ray flowers around the outer edge of the head and a central disc of many tiny five-lobed flowers. The whole affair is bright chrome-yellow and more or less flattened.

The ray flowers turn papery with age and fade to tan. They droop but remain attached. The plants flower almost all year long, so seed is generally available. *Baileya* is easy to grow; seed should be sown in the fall on gravelly soil in full sun and kept moist until the gray leaves are first visible. An occasional watering during winter dry periods is all that is needed to establish them. The coarse soil helps to hold the seed in place; once germination begins, any disturbance which re-orients the seed root anywhere but down can lead to the seedling's premature death. Plants two or three years old usually die during the summers but are generally replaced by ample younger progeny.

The plants are poisonous to sheep and goats. The foliage is not palatable but the flowers, which contain higher levels of the toxin, are.

Desert Marigold   Compositae   *Baileya multiradiata*

Fleabane

Although there are over thirty Fleabanes native to the Southwest, *Erigeron divergens* is by far the most common. It grows in open spaces at elevations between 1,000 and 9,000 feet throughout most of the western United States, extending its range into western Canada and northern Mexico.

It is a delicate wide-spreading annual or biennial herb, up to eighteen inches tall and as wide. The leaves are up to three-quarters of an inch long and may be strap-shaped with smooth margins, coarse lobes, or narrow feathery lobes cleft more than halfway to the stem. Stems and leaves are gray-green and covered with microscopic unbranched hairs.

As with the Desert Marigold, each stem tip carries a nodding head of buds or an erect expanded head of flowers. The heads are smaller, though; they are only three-eighths of an inch to a half-inch wide. The disc flowers are greenish yellow; the ray flowers are white, turning lavendar as they age. The tips of the rays are acute, not toothed as are those of *Baileya*. The plants flower from February to October, or later in warm areas.

Fleabane   Compositae   *Erigeron divergens*

Blue Flax

Blue Flax adapts to a wide range of climates and soils, occurring from Alaska to northern Mexico at elevations between 3,500 and 9,500 feet. Not a plant of low open desert, it is frequently found in the colder, higher deserts and arid grasslands of the Southwest. It is a true flax of the genus *Linum,* and some western tribes extracted fibers from the slender diffuse stems. Blue Flax is related to commercial flax, but its perennial habit and generally drier habitat set it apart.

The plants branch at the base; the stems, ten inches to a yard long, are closely invested for much of their length with narrowly spatulate or linear, obtuse leaves up to an inch long.

The only other branching occurs at the extreme tips of stems. Each such branch bears one to three satiny blue flowers with five petals, yellow at the base. The flowers are up to two inches across; in dry periods or sites the flowers are often somewhat smaller. After pollination, the petals drop off. The fruit is a globular capsule a quarter-inch in diameter that splits open at maturity.

The shimmering flowers are a welcome addition to the landscape designer's palette. Native-plant nurseries offer Blue Flax as gallon-sized plants which quickly naturalize, even in the low desert, if given a little supplemental water during the summer.

Blue Flax   Linaceae   *Linum lewisii*

Coulter's Hibiscus

Most people think of a hibiscus as a huge funnel-shaped scarlet bell tucked behind the ear of a maiden in the South Seas. The picture is accurate and lovely, but the Southwest offers its own unique species of hibiscus.

Coulter's Hibiscus is found in the southern half of Arizona, New Mexico and west Texas and in the Chihuahuan and Sonoran deserts of Mexico. It occurs between 1,500 and 4,500 feet on rocky slopes and in canyons. Flowering is from January to October.

The plant is an inconspicuous perennial, woody herb or sub-shrub up to three and a half feet tall, with few branches and sparse foliage. The herbage is bright green and covered with coarse, rough, branched hairs. Leaves are alternate, usually three-lobed and obtuse, about an inch long.

The flowers appear from leaf axils on slender stalks up to four inches long. Five overlapping petals with rounded rims form a deep cup or funnel up to an inch and three-quarters wide. The petals are pale yellow; sometimes the petal bases are crimson, giving the center of the flower a vibrant red glow.

Around the base of the ripening fruit radiate pointed sepals and sepal-like appendages that remain attached for a long time. The fruit is a globular capsule; inside are about a dozen fuzzy brown seeds, an eighth-inch in diameter. The capsule bursts into five parts, and the wind scatters the seeds.

Coulter's Hibiscus has been sporadically available at nurseries, but because of the twiggy, poor growth and appearance in a container, it has never attained the popularity it deserves. Even in the blast-furnace summer, when most wildflowers have long since caved in, Coulter's Hibiscus can happily bloom with a minimum of watering. It is well worth the effort to find and cultivate.

Coulter's Hibiscus   Malvaceae   *Hibiscus coulter*

Purple Groundcherry

Purple Groundcherry is a low-growing root perennial, at home from Kansas to northern Mexico and west to Nevada at elevations between 1,000 and 5,000 feet. It is common on the hard-packed fine-textured soils of mesas, plains and roadsides, especially where water stands from time to time. A sprawling plant with weak stems that branch mostly from the base, it is obscure except when in flower.

Leaves are alternate, with blades that taper to stalks that may be as long as the blades. All the herbage is covered in coarse granular hairs, giving it a grainy feeling.

The flowers usually occur in pairs from the leaf axils. They have an undulating surface and are shaped like wheels. The corolla is purple with a white center; from the center radiate five protruding anthers and a single greenish style.

The fruit, about three-eighths of an inch in diameter, gives the plant its other common name: Huskcherry. The berries are spherical, pulpy and with many seeds; each is enclosed in a close-fitting ribbed papery envelope. The protective envelope is actually the fused sepals, which enlarge to keep pace with the growth of the fruit.

A related, larger species from Mexico has been in cultivation since pre-Hispanic times. The fruit of that species is called a *tomatillo* and is widely available in Southwestern supermarkets. It is stewed, pureed into salsas with other condiments or sauteed lightly and served as a vegetable.

Purple Groundcherry   Solanaceae   *Physalis lobata*

Southwestern Ruellia

Winter kills many members of this genus, though a few introduced shrubby species are in horticultural use. But this native ruellia endures; while frost burns its herbaceous parts to the ground each winter, the perennial roots survive for many years.

Flowering is from April into October. Two inches long and slightly two-lipped, the purple flowers are held above the foliage in open leafless clusters at branch tips, between the forks of the branches.

The ascending stems are soft and weak and grow to a foot tall. Leaves are from an inch to five inches long, opposite, ovate, with stalks and rounded tips.

This ruellia is native to Mexico and to southern Arizona and Texas, growing in foothills and the deep soils of arroyo terraces and as a weed in fields. It has potential as a summer cultivar in desert habitats.

Southwestern Ruellia Acanthaceae *Ruellia nudiflora*

Saiya

Saiya is the name given *Amoreuxia palmatifida* by the Seri Indians of Sonora. There is no English common name for the plants, though a yellow-flowered relative from Texas is known as Yellow-show. Another name from eastern Sonora is *Temaqui*, of supposed Opata Indian origin.

Saiya is one of Arizona's most strikingly handsome species. It is a summer root perennial from the rocky grassland slopes of the Mexican border region, growing at elevations between 3,500 and 5,000 feet.

The single stems are six inches to a foot tall; the leaves are an inch and a half wide and look like tiny, jagged palm trees. Frequently the green leaves are tinged bronze by the sun.

Tuberous and edible, the root is frequently misshapen due to the rocky soil. The roots are the size of Jerusalem artichokes and have the same texture and taste. The Seris eat the roots raw, baked, or boiled with deer meat or turtle fat.

The flowers are two and a half inches wide and consist of five bright orange-yellow petals. Four of the petals are blotched at the base with bright red and grouped to one side. The fifth petal lacks the red blotch and extends away from the other four. Two sets of incurving stamens reverse the theme; on the side with four petals is a set of stamens with yellow anthers, opposing a set with purple anthers on the side with the single petal.

The flower is "buzz pollinated" by large bees. The bees land on the center of the flower and vibrate their wings vigorously, shaking pollen onto their bodies. Cross-pollination results when the bee sheds some of the pollen with another buzz at the next flower.

The elliptical fruit, an inch and a half long, is unique and edible. As it ripens, the outer, opaque layer dries and falls off, revealing a parchment-like, translucent inner layer. Visible inside are the comma-shaped seeds.

Although rarely cultivated, Saiya has a high potential for exploitation in the semi-arid summer-rainfall areas of the Southwest.

Saiya   Bixaceae   *Amoreuxia palmatifida*

Dune Evening Primrose

Although *Oenothera deltoidea* occurs on dunes throughout the Southwest and northern Mexico, any sandy, well-drained soil in full sun will support a colony of these handsome annual or biennial plants. After wet winters, great tracts of western desert are blotched from February to May with extensive strands of this sweet-scented wildling.

The plants sometimes grow to a height of three feet, but eighteen inches is more usual. There is one erect central stem and a half-dozen or so branches from the base. The branches are more or less declining, and curl inward as they dry; the leafless frameworks they leave in the sand persist for several years. Locals refer to these remains as bird cages or baskets.

The leaves are pointed oblongs with extreme variations in shape, size, and degree and kind of teeth on the margins. Leaves are from a quarter of an inch to three inches long.

The white flowers originate in the axils of the leaves of the upper half of the plants. They begin as nodding buds, enveloped in pointy sepals with purple spots and glandular hairs. The flowers are two and a half to three and a half inches wide and form a plate or shallow bowl, attached to the top of the fruit by a slender tube an inch or two long. The fruit is a capsule an inch or two long, shaped like a slender beak.

The Dune Evening Primrose is not known to be in cultivation. Providing its habitat requirements, if they can be duplicated, should lead to success in growing it.

Dune Evening Primrose   Onagraceae   *Oenothera deltoidea*

Purple Mat

As the name implies, Purple Mat is a low-growing plant with rich purple flowers. It is common throughout most of the Southwest and from the southwestern edge of the Great Plains into southeastern California. Given a wet winter and spring, these annuals can form carpets of rich red-purple a foot or two in diameter and six inches to twelve inches high. In dry years the plants may produce only one or two leaves and a single flower.

The flowers are up to a half-inch long and shaped like funnels, with yellow throats and flaring, rounded five-lobed corollas. The five stamens are about half as long as the corolla and are attached at different levels in the throat of the flower.

Microscopic white hairs, short and stiff and with swollen bases, cover the plant and give it a coarse texture. There are three described varieties, differing only in the character of the hairs on the leaves. The leaves are a half-inch to two and a half inches long, medium to dark green. They are alternately arranged, but appear to be in clusters at branch junctions. Leaves have a strong central vein, a smooth margin, a rounded tip and generally taper toward the base.

Habitats include roadsides, open desert plains, gravelly arroyo bottoms and terraces, and, to a lesser extent, rocky slopes.

Purple Mat   Hydrophyllaceae   *Nama hispidum*

Desert Zinnia

This root-suckering perennial sub-shrub has little in common with its close relative, the bright garden-variety annual zinnia. *Zinnia acerosa* colonizes rocky desert hillsides and dry mesas and can be the dominant understory shrub with palo verdes and the ubiquitous creosote bush. Its range is from southwestern Texas to southern Arizona and northern Mexico, at elevations between 2,000 and 5,000 feet. Between April and October, the plant flowers profusely.

As with other members of the Sunflower family, the blossoms actually contain two types of flowers: five to seven white ray flowers and bright yellow protruding disc flowers. The elegant ray flowers turn downward and are rounded to oblong, a half-inch in diameter. Remaining attached, the rays age to tan and give the impression that the plant is in flower most of the time.

The plant grows as a compact rounded shrub, densely leafy. The leaves are gray-green, a half-inch to three-quarters of an inch long and linear in shape, with smooth margins. Minute unbranched white hairs cover the leaves.

The plants are sometimes available as nursery stock from specialty growers. They make excellent cover for bare, scraped cement-like caliche if not overwatered in the summer heat. Some watering is necessary to establish the plants and to get them to spread.

Desert Zinnia   Compositae   *Zinnia acerosa*

Fairy Duster

Fairy Duster is a shrub, one to three feet tall, with powder-puff flowers similar to those of the miniature mimosas of the South. As with much of the pea and bean family, the leaves are bipinnately compound, made up of many leaflets arranged symmetrically. Leaves are dark green and minutely hairy, as are the twigs.

About four to seven flowers cluster at branch tips to form the creamy to intense-pink puffs. Each flower has a five-lobed corolla a sixteenth of an inch long, slender filaments united into groups, tiny sepals and a pistil that resembles a stamen except that it is a little stouter and has a globular stigma at its tip.

The bean-like fruit is about two inches long and three-eights of an inch wide. It is flat and pointed, with a raised rib on the margin. The fruit is explosive, splitting from the tip and recoiling with enough force to catapult the seed, a hard brownish-tan egg-shaped disc, some distance from the parent plant.

Fairy Duster is an efficient soil stabilizer, and has become popular for landscaping in the Southwest. It tolerates browsing well; livestock find it tasty and, because of its size and abundance, it is common in the diet of desert deer.

Fairy Duster   Leguminosae   *Calliandra eriophylla*

Magenta Four O'Clock

This is another of the region's hard-to-miss natives. Mounds of weak blue-green stems and leaves tinged with purple, plants may grow to a yard across and six feet high, if supported on other vegetation. The plant is a perennial herb, growing from a tuberous root up to three feet long and two inches in diameter. The roots may be sparingly branched.

At the tips of the stems are bell-shaped whorls of specialized leaves called involucres. Each involucre is about an inch long, has five coarse teeth and protects two to eight developing buds. The buds develop at different rates, so that only one or two flowers are open from each involucre at a time.

The purple-red flowers are an inch wide. Each corolla has five very shallow lobes and encloses five whitish-yellow stamens. The stamens are united at the base but free from one another for most of their length. The stamens and the single magenta style protrude from the corolla mouth. Shaped like footballs, the brown, ribbed fruits are about a quarter-inch long.

Leaves are opposite, triangular, acute to obtuse at the tip and rounded or cordate at the base. Blades are up to two inches long and three inches wide; stalks are slender, from a half-inch long to as long as the blade. Leaves formed toward the flowering stem tips are much smaller than basal leaves.

Magenta Four O'Clock is related to the common garden four o'clock and has recently made its way into cultivation in the Southwest. It is easily grown from cuttings or seeds.

Hopi Indians ingest the roots to induce visions, and the powdered root has been used as a treatment for stomach-ache. It is best to admire the plant without sampling it, though; its cultivated relative is poisonous and causes stomach pain, diarrhea and vomiting.

Magenta Four O'Clock   Nyctaginaceae   *Mirabilis multiflora*

Terms

Areole—A modified branch system in which the leaves appear as spines or tufts of hair, appearing in regular patterns on all cacti.

Axil—The angle formed between the upper side of a leaf or twig and the stem from which it grows.

Bract—A modified leaf, often scalelike, usually located at the base of a fruit or flower.

Calyx—The outer whorl of leaves at the base of a flower.

Corolla—The petals of a flower.

Cuticle—A thick waxy coating, found on many cacti.

Deciduous—Falling off at maturity.

Glochid—Fine hairlike barbed spines, found in areoles.

Inflorescence—An arrangement of flowers clustered on a plant.

Lobed—Having margins that are indented. The indentations do not reach to the center or base.

Perianth—The envelope of a flower, particularly where the calyx and corolla cannot be distinguished.

Petiole—The stalk of a leaf that attaches it to the stem.

Rosette—A crowded, circular cluster of leaves. Often appears to grow directly out of the ground.

Tubercle—A raised knob or nipple-like protruberance from the fleshy body of a cactus.

Appendix

View along the Gila (*Cereus giganteus*) circa 1859

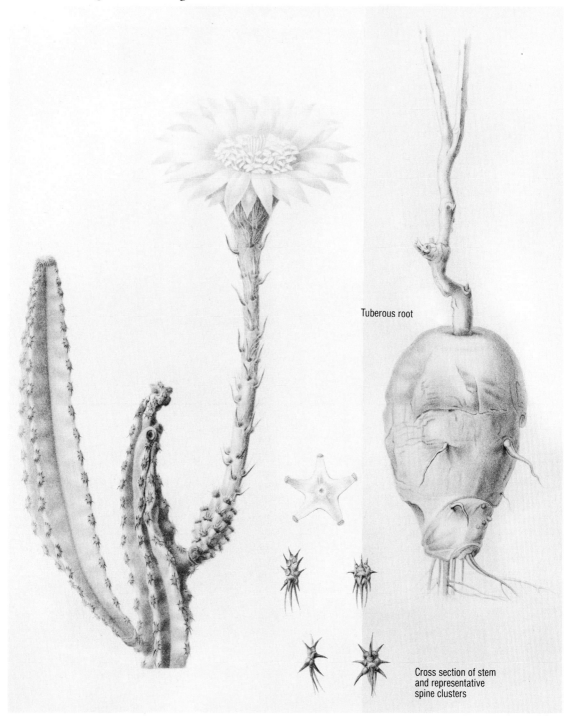

Tuberous root

Cross section of stem
and representative
spine clusters

It is sometimes difficult to distinguish between barrel cacti and Saguaros, particularly between young Saguaros and tall, old barrels. Barrel cacti may reach a height of eleven feet, but the following features set them apart:

	SAGUARO	COMMON LARGE BARREL CACTI
Central spines	round cross-section; straight	flat cross-section; hooked in some species
Spines	no minute ridges across width	minute ridges across width
Ribs	straight	slightly spiraling
Stems	narrowest near base	widest at base
Flowers	white	yellow, red, orange
Fruit	spiny; green flushed with red; splitting open from top	no spines; yellow; not splitting open from top

Detail and horizontal section of Saguaro

Wislizen's Barrel

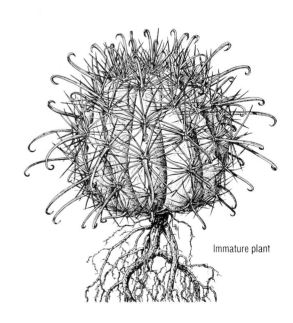

Spines common to non-flowering portions

Flutes or outer ribs

Water storage tissue

Pulp

SECTION A-A

Ribs of the woody skeleton

Areoles

Central spines

Areoles approx. 1 inch apart

Immature plant

FIG. 4. SAGUARO

MATURE SPINE
CLUSTER

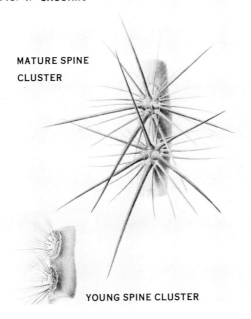

YOUNG SPINE CLUSTER

FIG. 5. WISLIZEN'S BARREL

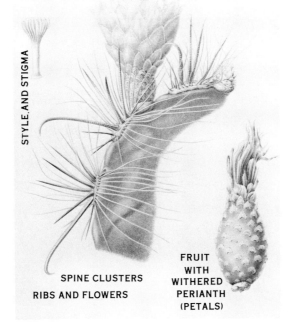

STYLE AND STIGMA

SPINE CLUSTERS

RIBS AND FLOWERS

FRUIT
WITH
WITHERED
PERIANTH
(PETALS)

FIG. 7. CORKY-SEED PINCUSHION

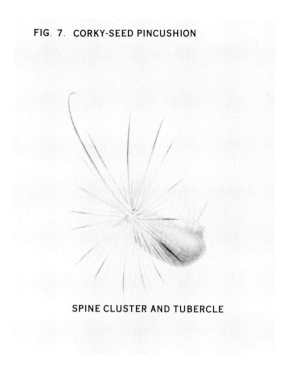

SPINE CLUSTER AND TUBERCLE

Chainfruit Cholla

Stem and fruits

Purple Prickly Pear

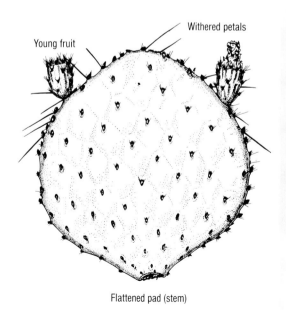

Young fruit

Withered petals

Flattened pad (stem)

FIG. 8. ENGELMANN'S HEDGEHOG
SINGLE STEM

FRUIT BEFORE SPINES FALL OFF

Pollination of the Soaptree Yucca

On still, humid summer nights one of the most complex relationships in nature reveals itself. The moths emerge from pupating in the earth and mate in flight. Then the females seek out flowers within the massive inflorescence of the yucca. The moth collects pollen from a number of stamens and works it into a ball, held securely under her chin as she clambers about within the flowers. When she has gathered enough pollen, the moth climbs to the ovulary and carefully packs the ball into a pore at its tip and thus pollinates the flower.

The moth is not altruistic in providing this service. After depositing the ball of pollen, she carefully inserts her egg- laying tube into the ovulary and deposits her eggs next to the future seeds. Later, as the fruit develops, the eggs hatch and the larvae begin to feed on the seeds. The larvae eventually exit through the ripening fruit wall and fall to the ground to burrow in, pupate and await the renewal of the cycle.

There are many seeds, so the few eaten by the larvae are not a serious loss. Indeed, without the moth's help, there would be very little seed. In areas where the moths are not found, no seed is set. The pollen is too heavy to be spread by the wind, and the architecture of the flower is unsuited to pollination by other organisms such as bees or birds.

Yucca moth gathering pollen

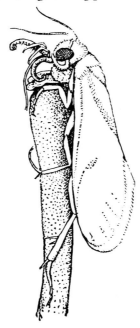

Terminology Describing Leaves

Shapes

Linear   Elliptical   Spatulate   Ovate   Obovate   Lanceolate

Bases

Acute   Rounded   Cordate

Tips

Acute   Obtuse

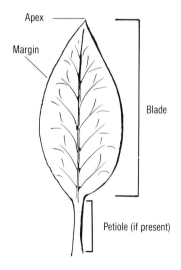

Apex
Margin
Blade
Petiole (if present)

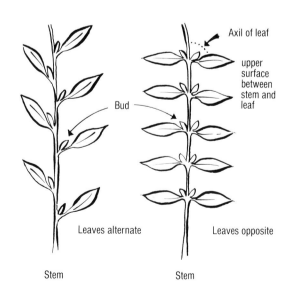

Axil of leaf
upper surface between stem and leaf
Bud
Leaves alternate
Leaves opposite
Stem
Stem

116

Longitudinal section of flower

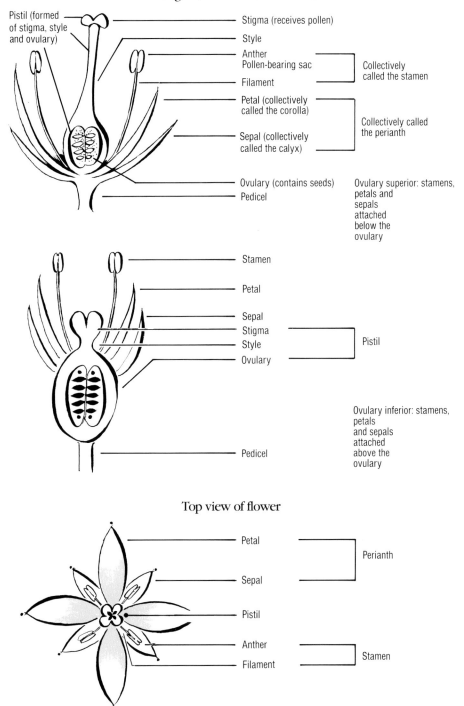

Pistil (formed of stigma, style and ovulary)

Stigma (receives pollen)

Style

Anther
Pollen-bearing sac

Filament

Collectively called the stamen

Petal (collectively called the corolla)

Sepal (collectively called the calyx)

Collectively called the perianth

Ovulary (contains seeds)

Pedicel

Ovulary superior: stamens, petals and sepals attached below the ovulary

Stamen

Petal

Sepal

Stigma

Style

Ovulary

Pistil

Ovulary inferior: stamens, petals and sepals attached above the ovulary

Pedicel

Top view of flower

Petal

Sepal

Perianth

Pistil

Anther

Filament

Stamen

Desert Hen-and-Chicks

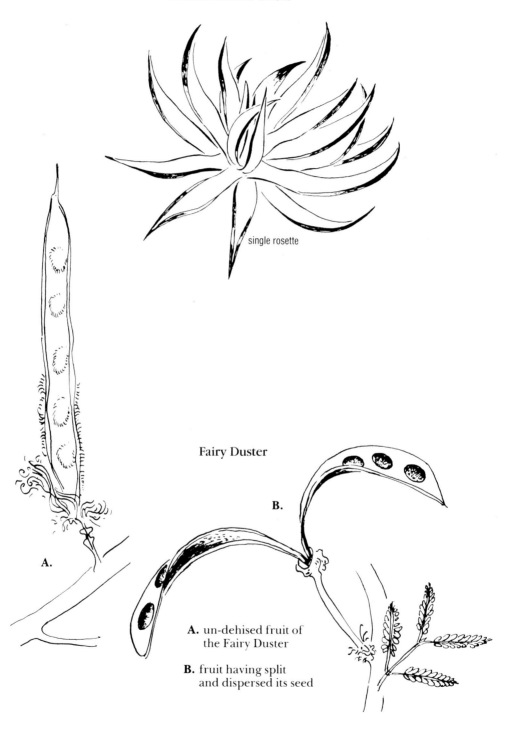

single rosette

Fairy Duster

B.

A.

A. un-dehised fruit of
the Fairy Duster

B. fruit having split
and dispersed its seed

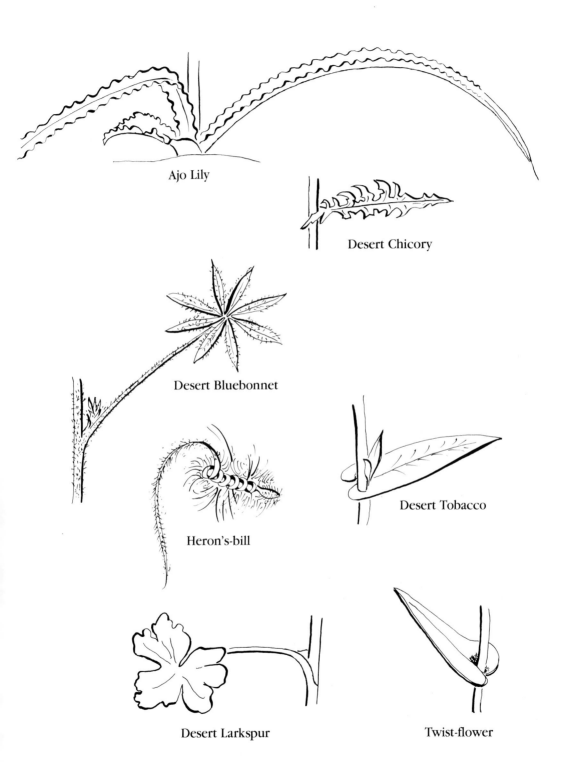

Ajo Lily

Desert Chicory

Desert Bluebonnet

Heron's-bill

Desert Tobacco

Desert Larkspur

Twist-flower

Acknowledgements

The illustrations on pages 110, 111, 113, and the page-114 details of Corky-seed Pincushion and Engelmann's Hedgehog are reproduced from *Report on United States and Mexican Boundary Survey, Volume II,* 1859.

The Saguaro detail on page 112 is reproduced with permission from *Raymond Carlson's The Flowering Cactus,* McGraw-Hill Book Co., 1954.

The illustration of the Wislizen's Barrel on page 112 is reproduced with permission from Lyman Benson's *The Cacti of Arizona,* University of Arizona Press, 1969, as are the details of the Chainfruit Cholla and Purple Prickly Pear on page 114.

The illustration on page 115 is reproduced from *Annals of the Missouri Botanical Garden Annual Report 1989.*

The illustrations of leaf shapes on page 116 are reproduced from *Webster's New World Dictionary, College Edition,* 1958.